COUNT ON
YOUR FINGERS
AFRICAN STYLE

COUNT ON YOUR FINGERS AFRICAN STYLE

by Claudia Zaslavsky

Illustrated by Jerry Pinkney

Thomas Y. Crowell   New York

Text copyright © 1980 by Claudia Zaslavsky
Illustrations copyright © 1980 by Jerry Pinkney
For information address Thomas Y. Crowell Junior Books, 10 East 53rd Street,
New York, N.Y. 10022. Published simultaneously in Canada by
Fitzhenry & Whiteside Limited, Toronto.

Library of Congress Cataloging in Publication Data
Zaslavsky, Claudia.
Count on your fingers African style.
SUMMARY: Describes how finger counting is used
for communication of price and quantity in an
East African market place.
1. Mathematics, Primitive—Africa, Sub-Saharan—
Juvenile literature. 2. Numeration—Juvenile litera-
ture. [1. Mathematics, Primitive—Africa, Sub-Saharan.
2. Number systems. 3. Africa—Social life and customs]
I. Pinkney, Jerry. II. Title.
GN645. Z37 1980   513   77-26586
ISBN 0-690-03864-X   ISBN 0-690-03865-8 lib. bdg.
1 2 3 4 5 6 7 8 9 10
First Edition

COUNT ON
YOUR FINGERS
AFRICAN STYLE

A Note from the Author

People all over the world count on their fingers. Perhaps you do, too. People in Africa, as well as in other places, have special ways of finger counting. In this book you will read about some of these ways. If you were to go to Africa tomorrow, you would find that some people use finger counting, while others do not.

Each year more and more African children attend schools that are very much like yours. All the children learn to speak a language common to their region. Usually it is different from their own. In parts of East Africa the language is Swahili. In other places it is English, or French, or Portuguese, or Arabic, or some other language commonly spoken in Africa. As more people in Africa learn to speak more languages, the need for finger counting in markets will become less.

People often use finger counting because it is their custom. But when children go to school, they learn ways that are different from those of their parents. When I was in Africa, I asked many students how their people counted on their fingers. Some knew very well how to do it. Others said, "I will ask my father," or "I will ask my grandmother."

Probably nothing will ever replace finger counting entirely. After all, fingers make such a handy calculator—they are always with you!

Claudia Zaslavsky

1

You are in a faraway land.

    You are in East Africa.

Today is a market day.

People come from near and far to

    buy all sorts of things—food,

    cloth, pots, beads.

Market day is a great event.

People meet friends they have not

    seen for many days.

Some tell funny stories. Others have

    sad news to give their friends.

People speak in excited voices as

    they buy and sell.

Everyone tries to get the best price.

Some people are waving their

    fingers as they talk.

You join the crowd.

An orange would taste good

on a hot day like this.

You decide to buy three, so you can

keep two for later.

But how can you say that you want

three oranges?

You speak only English.

You don't hear anyone speaking English.

Well, what can you do?

You can use your fingers.

You can point to the oranges,

  and show three on your fingers.

But how will you do it?

  This way...

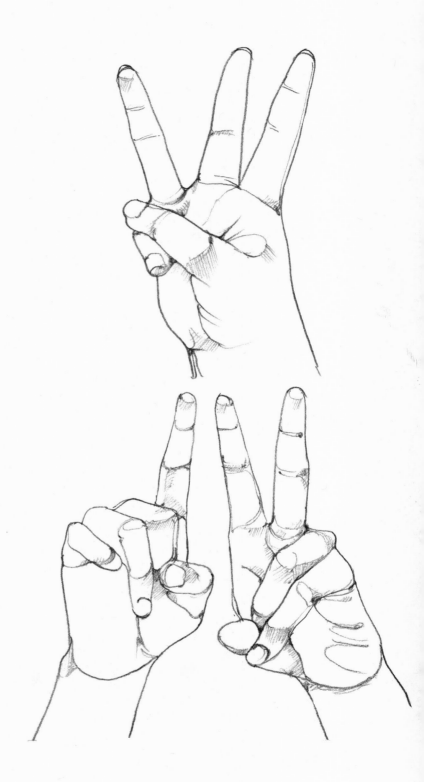

  or this way...?

Go to the orange seller

  and see what happens.

It works! She gives you three oranges.

Now she asks you for *itatu* cents—

    one penny for each orange.

This is how the Kamba people

    show three on their fingers.

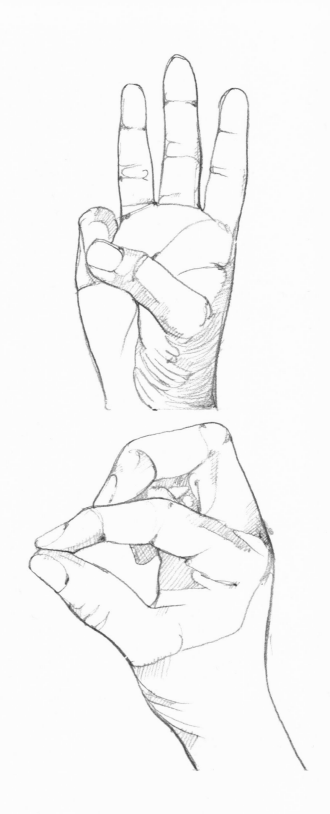

Three Maasai boys are looking

    at the oranges.

They talk to one another and laugh.

One boy shows this sign

    with his right hand.

How many oranges does he want?

The market woman gives him three

    oranges, too.

The Kamba people and the Maasai people
live near each other in a country
called Kenya.

The Maasai buy things like pots
and knives from the Kamba.

The Kamba buy cows and beads
from the Maasai.

But they speak different languages.

They can say how many they want
and how much money to pay
with finger counting.

Now you see some ripe yellow bananas.

The Kamba farmer picked them

    just this morning.

How can you show that you want

    eight bananas?

This way...

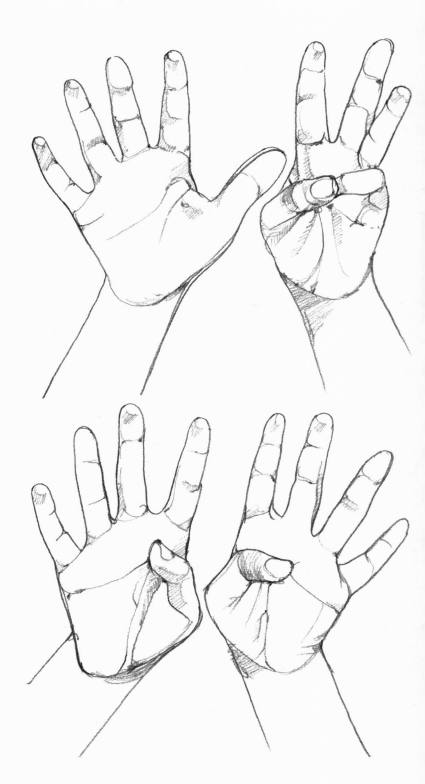

or this way...

or some other way?

This is the Kamba sign for eight.
The right hand holds three fingers
     of the left hand.
Five fingers on the right and three
     fingers on the left make eight.
The Kamba word for eight is *nyaanya*.

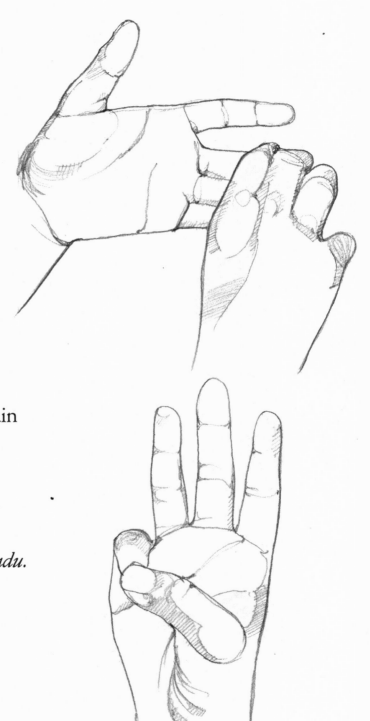

The Taita people also live in Kenya.
From his farm this Taita farmer can see
     Mount Kilimanjaro, the tallest mountain
     in Africa.
The Taita sign for three is just like
     the Kamba sign.
The Taita word is almost the same. It is *idadu*.
The Kamba word is *itatu*.
Can you guess what number the Taita
     farmer is showing?

14

That is the Taita sign for eight.

Four fingers and four fingers make eight.

The Taita word for eight is *munani*.

It means four and four.

What beautiful beads!

The Maasai women make these colorful
necklaces while the men and boys take care
of the cattle.

The man wants you to buy one.

How many shillings does he ask for it?

He waves the four fingers of his right
    hand.

What can he mean?

Eight shillings is the price of the beads.

Why does he wave four fingers?

Perhaps to show that four and four make
  eight.

All these people live in the same
  country in East Africa.

They all live in Kenya.

Yet they all have different ways of showing eight
  on their fingers. Kamba…Taita…Maasai…

Very small children in Africa play

    finger games and learn to count

    on their fingers.

Didn't you? Did you say:

"This little pig went to market.

This little pig stayed at home.

This little pig ate roast beef.

This little pig had none.

This little pig cried all the way home."

Little children in Africa learn finger

    games from their big brothers and sisters.

They bend the fingers of the left hand
   with the right thumb as they say:
"This is little finger.
This is the big brother of little finger.
This is long finger.

This one picks up the food.
This is the bent thumb."

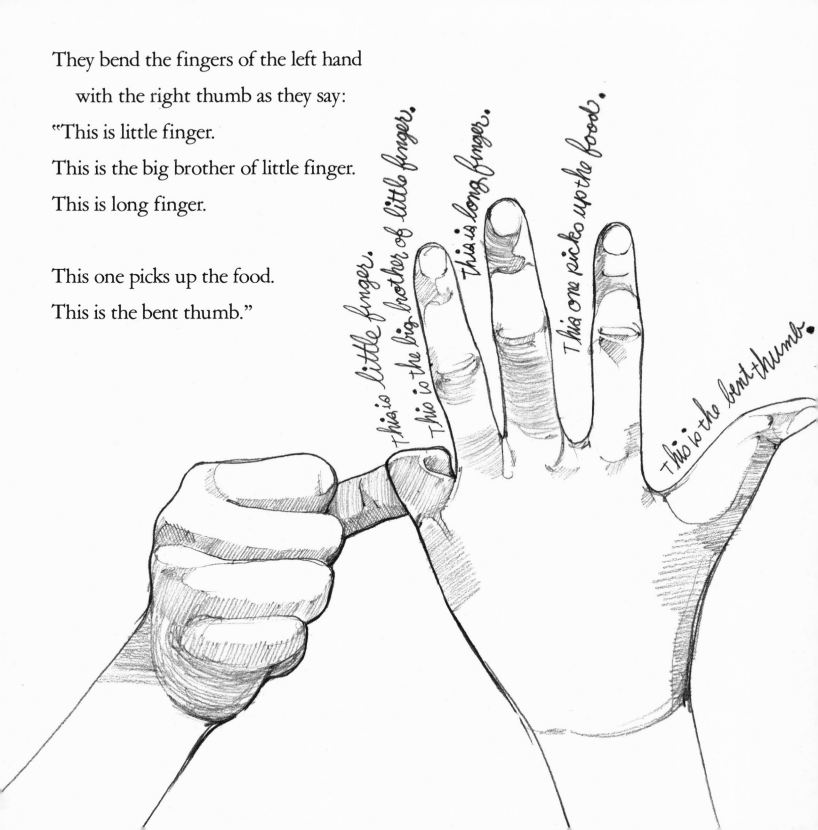

Here is the story of the fingers

    that cry out:

"Nye! Nye! Nye!"

"What's the matter?"

"He's hungry!"

"The food is in the pot."

"Let's eat it!"

"When Mommy comes home, I'll tell!"

All over the world children and grown-ups
   sometimes use their fingers for counting.
   Don't you?

Fatu can show you her way.
Fatu lives in Sierra Leone,
   a country in West Africa.
Often she helps her mother sell bright red
   tomatoes.
She calls out: "Tomatoes! Fresh tomatoes!"

Fatu has twenty tomatoes in her basin.

Her mother laid them down as Fatu counted

them on her fingers.

That way she knew just how many she had.

This is how Fatu counted the tomatoes.

She bent one finger for each tomato.

First she bent the fingers of her left

hand, starting with the little finger.

Then she counted from six to ten on her

right hand, starting with the

little finger.

For eleven to twenty, she did the same

thing all over again.

Some of Fatu's people count from
eleven to twenty on their toes.
Her people, the Mende, have a special
word for twenty.
It is *nu gboyongo.*
It means a whole person.
All ten fingers and all ten toes
have been counted.

Fatu's mother does not need to count
on her fingers.

She can do even the biggest sums
in her head.
Fatu will be able to do that too when
she is older.

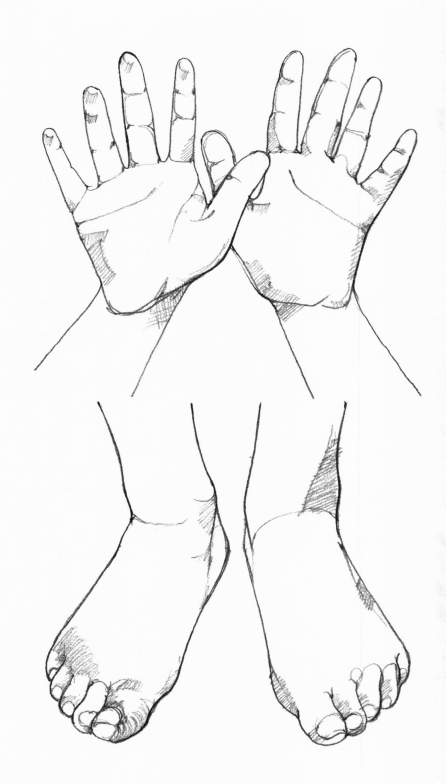

28

Do you know that some of our English
    number words are named for finger counting?
Eleven means one left.
Count out all ten fingers.
Then you will need one more to reach
    eleven.
Twelve means two left over, after counting
    all ten fingers.

Many people in South Africa show
    six by holding up the right thumb.
The Zulu people live in South Africa.
Isithipa is the Zulu word for six.
    It means take the thumb.

Isishiyagalombili means leave out
two fingers.

Can you guess what number that is?

It is the Zulu word for eight.
The word tells how many fingers
are not used.

People all over the world count
on their fingers.

Their number names prove it!

Can you make up your own finger signs
for the numbers from one to ten?

Ask your friends to guess which numbers
you are showing.

Then make up new number names to go
with your signs.